This book belongs to:

Name: _____

Date: _____

Contact: _____

Cover art: 'One Horse' by Lara Katz, 14.
Photograph published in *Stone Soup* Magazine, April 2018.

Stone Soup, founded in 1973, is published by
Children's Art Foundation—Stone Soup Inc., a
nonprofit organization based in the Unted States.
Find out more at Stonesoup.com.

StoneSoup

www.ingramcontent.com/pod-product-compliance
Lightning Source LLC
Chambersburg PA
CBHW072007290426
44109CB00018B/2157